GOAT TROUBLES

GOAT TROUBLES

and other CHICAGO Poems

John Ross

John Ross

To order additional copies of this book, contact:
Xlibris Corporation
1-888-795-4274
www.Xlibris.com
Orders@Xlibris.com
78304

Contents

Third: On Behalf of Lovable Losers

Home: Cross-Town lovers

Dedication:

To the honor
of Chicago
prima-poet:
        Carl Sandburg.

and
dedicated
to the Rev.
        Gail Tapscott.

It was she, who
first allured
me to this firmly
planted town.

I am also grateful
to Professor
        Peter Gilmour,

who helped me
trimly mark,
some notes

and breaks,
in watching
Midwest sound.

It is hopeless
for the occasional
visitor to try
to keep up with Chicago—
she out grows her
prophecies faster than she
can make them.

She is always a novelty;
for she is never
the Chicago you saw
when you passed
through the last time.

—*Mark Twain "Life on the Mississippi", 1883*

First.

Goat Troubles

"The lust of the goat is the bounty of God"
—William Blake

CITING CARL SANDBURG

(a poem loosely based on several of his celebrated quotes)

I.
LIKE HIM, I too brood about
things, with my lap top in the corner
of
        an L train;

rarely making a mistake in
verse but mostly in life, and
then having to face
it
        head on.

Avoiding religion and philosophy,
largely since they would be solid
work, hours spent in a world partly
primate
        to me.

Choosing to carve poetry instead,
like a sea animal living on land
wanting to swim
into
        thin air.

I search for complex prosody to
solve, typing up a phantom
text
        which tells

why rainbows are complete, and
why they simply choose
to
        go away.

I will construct villanelles and a
few clouds, wage a war on
my screen, and then no one really
cares to

      scroll down.

II.
Even stranger, lake winds
blow through my Rogers Park
window. They
are
      just shy

of splitting a dozen or
more poets and romantic
minds
      in me;

and I don't know how to
interpret any one of them.
But they do try
to
      spin that

I am an idealist, while
masking myself a
theologian, having belief
in   everything,

then solving for proofs.
They tell me that it's a
harsh millennium, I should not
be
      an optimist

while opening my eyes
and then waking
in
        the morning.

But poets can only unbolt,
then slam a few doors,
forcing we
who
        glimpse through

to guess
about what may be seen
at
        any instant.

III.
While reciting my e.e. cummings
I require no
coach, the verses
they
        are enough.

But there's a serious deviation
between him and say Milton;
and dare I
guess:
        Mr. Shakespeare.

They pen on about paradise,
and yet never spent a day
or a moment over there
in
        any wonder.

Oh! And Dante too, fingering his
dreadful: *L'inferno*, never heard
or smelled any sulfur drops
or
       hellish Bible fears!

But like Carl Sandburg, I
can write volumes about
Chicago, after breathing the
town over
for
       months, then years.

TOP OF THE SEARS OR HAVE YOU, THE WILLIS

Oh.
And should
you take the
time to go up
there, the prospect
is something only
Manhattan will boast
serving up to tourists
in the best of earthenware
and goblets. Well they're amiss.
Simply, amiss. There's some peculiar magic in
not seeing a Central Park below, but some geometric
grid all decked out like an architect building bungalows *overtime.*

WINGING DOWN DEVON

Traveling due west from Sheridan
you're ever amazed at the blocks
and blocks of multitudes.

Every time hauler bus 36 stops,
you can fetch on-or-off to some
inn-keeper nation.

You reset your watch, as your dart rider flits
past dozens of chromatic sari's in
sequential view ports every twelve yards or so.

Unsure of India or Pakistan the
enchantment is still quite novel.
And so you glimpse a few bookstores, boasting

their sales that week in glib Arabic,
and you notice how that namesake hardware
store still seems to compete for

parking space near the corner
at Clark and Devon. Three Sisters Café,
Kosher bakeshops & Rosenblum's Bookstore

help elevate Jerusalem salads,
hummus and cold sodas to the brain.
Then you suddenly yield you're way out.

It's scorching now, you're on foot in untried
lands, and diet coke still has
some *bona fide* American clout.

So you drink quietly taking in how
Ecuadorians, P.R.'s and Cubans
shop for the same Latin

coffee blends and Goya brands
on tumble-down shelves.
From time to time you hear quip

argots of Spanish, along with
every other sentence
jumping ear to ear with: *si, si!*

After only a block or five,
air-cooled 36 joined east/west at
quondam Church Street,

now gathers you in all over again.
Far away and up for many more
blocks and blocks, and blocks,

then dangles you finally to finish
by the Argo Georgian
Deli, then trims you swiftly

back again then forwards,
with only a Cubs cap,
lay over time,

and a box of Russian pastry
as your modest little carry-on.

YOUNG PRESIDENT FROM ILLINOIS

There's a daring men in town of both solid sound,
one of change and one of quell.

There's a daring men in town of both residence twill,
one of recruit and one of exit.

There's a daring men in town of both united toilets,
one of hither and one of thither.

There's a daring men in town of both potable fountains,
one of color and one of pale.

There's a daring men in town of both yellow jitneys,
one of ours and one of theirs.

There's a daring men in town of both restless shadow,
one of sheets and one of coal.

And now he's a whistlin' in an oval office!
He's whistlin' in a tweed home away from home!

He's white and his spirit is blacken.
He's black and his house is whiten.

Takin' measures from Kenya and a city in Jakarta, now our
'Hog butcher for the world' has something even greater to say!

GOAT TROUBLES

Oh. Once again, he
Simply *won't* move.
Then again we can't

Even cipher the problem.
He's been to clinic. He's been to vet.
No fever. He's eating again though.

Everything in port of lake, he's been eating.
Buying everything, still donning his red
& blue. Spun-up and down in cap and gown.

It seems. No stomach problems.
Then it seems. No profligate self.
He's been to clinic. He's been to vet.

He's been to soothsayer.
He's been to shrink.
First, second, and third, every trials been tried.

Home doctor's opinion has never been taken to heed.
They've examined and examined and also scanned.
A hundred years now, tailing and watching and hoping . . .

And still no clear diagnosis. No therapeutic end.
X-rays and urine. Then blood and microscopes.
MRI.'s and MMPI's seem . . . *virtuoso!*

But, once again he just won't *move.*
He won't even *budge.*
They just can't seem to figure the problem.

Even his tall mallow is smooth. Yes, it's smooth.
Be it metropolis, Springfield or the on lake.
Be it chewing gum, GN or the office in the front.

Is he *to* be or *not* to be even a proper dug out question?
He just won't step . . . and even with an intravenous hoof.
And sometimes then, you just can't ever, ever figure things out to be.

He's been to soothsayer.
He's been to shrink.
First, second and third, every test's been taken.

THE TASTE

Hugging near the band shell
Of sweet famine, with
The eyes of aroma, too many pitched

Tables, soft palates and tongues
keep passing by for samples.

Then harder palates, and the
Epiglottis, come charging
Even further with eating house fables as each
One enters. Every one enters in need.

Suburbanized, tripped
and thirsty, streaming thickeners

With rolls of printed tickets
And saucy texture, they come to taste and nibble.
Their receptors puckered by
Labeled booths and lined tables.

Cooling and fretting by the lake,
they seem but a summer clock

For rubbernecks in Grant
Park. Overwhelming the city as led by a
Trance, forever they salvo the
Summer on and on and on and

To infinity, they keep on coming
and pending for a costly fee.

Departing from city hall's first
Big annual feast:
In honor of
Hungrier Mayor Bilandic.

They just keep fleshing out from
tongue to tongue and state by state,

Nearby thrashing from
Wisconsin, Indiana, Michigan . . .
And some say even saltier coasts:
Atlantic.

DOWNTOWN GROMMET

TOward.........the LOop and *on* the LooP,
ThrOugh..........the loop,
Then under . . . the LOoP.
AcrOssss.........the looOOoop. *Now* . . . **Suuupra** the LOOp, the '**L**' is buzzzzing

chesty up >>>tow*ard*

heaven
where
the vista
is *neck-ruff!*

AND where else
can you
study a sculpture garden *al fresco,*
for the dubious fare of a turnstile?

Gliding, gliding,
Peering
down through the summit of
a braggart
window?
AND with a wayward visitor
gliding, gliding, next to you
adrift?
THEN
slickly,
slickly peering astray?
WANDERING politely back again.
Pleading, pleading, earnest:
hand-picking for your Midwestern compass. "O*range* or,
cherry?
Lime or *plum?*" YOU offer him. EACH branch
is tourist juicy.

QUOTABLE ARCHITECTURE

"Only the Oracular."
Some will say that the edifice is in Chicago's temper; that
Spatial posture is in the order to design:

Sophisticated
Oracular
Modern.

They say its those aliens! It's they who zap things out like:
"Well, I guess sky scraping does have a certain . . . genesis here!"

And: *"Form usually backsides some kind of function"* with
"More is by far, far, far—the less" trickling from
The mouths of many visas. Yes, that's what they say far, far, far away about this town.

Such hearsay has it that our high rise became: *"the space wonder of the modern age,"*
And: that *"Every jazzy landscape now wizards all the commerce in this American city."*
That's what they say, I've heard it . . . whatever it means.

And also that: "*Gangster wherewithal still bank rolls every go-ahead
So, upright and perpendicular geometry can mirror the streetwise grid."*
Wow—they say some say that too? Okay! If truth be told, I may have just read it somewhere.

Yet, I did hear an old sociology prof from Poland plainly declare: *"Chicago is all about a
Midwestern-American Axis, simply shouldering its working class manners."*
Although I clearly heard it—I admit, It was second hand from someone at Northeastern
Illinois University (*not* Northwestern).

But yesterday, I personally did witness a visiting (British) LaSalle Street banker. Glibly he
quipped to me:
"Those buildings do seem quite confident of one another way, way up there, don't they?"
He was glancing up at the goddess Ceres while he appeared to be trading on his Blackberry.

Then, just this very morning, I heard two visitors from Copenhagen utter with Danish accents:
"Oh yes, there's . . . trading grandeur in Chicago . . . reminds one of the Borsen!"
I heard two other Scandinavian guests chat on about the primacy of the Sears, then on and
on about . . . .

The Cathedral of Christ the Light, and our awkward matching of a mausoleum with corporate
office space.
"But . . . that's in Oakland, California!," I ultimately blasted back . . . I'm sorry, but I had to
let them know.
Spatial posture is in the ordering to design:

Skidmore
Owings
Merrill.

That's what they say: **SOM**(E).

OAK STREET BEACH

This little strip will hold narrow
                    wet
                    rain.

A sandpaper lining that welcomes day workers with
                    beach
                    balls,

Which then requires them missing from their jobs on the
                    Mag
                    Mile.

It tugs them distant from their work path and pushes
                    them
                    next,

Away from their desks high up in their sky-chafers, and down onto the
                    sands
                    below.

Such roustabouts will plow and crop all day if you punch for them their
                    running
                    meters.

They like to drift away twice daily then return back again to work a bit less
                    hungry,
                    thirsty.

Direful, missing the tan and volleys they caught downstairs sunning on
                    dropping
                    light.

This supplanted freshwater coastal brim gathers lakeside workers for
simple
furloughs;

Then cheats the foolish office clock high up, with nothing but lengthy
stolen
breaks.

LITHUANICA

Sometimes I perch upon locomotion
from Midway, on board the orange line
and
take charge, dancing toward
a trig-trimmed visit to a little Lithuanian lair.

By hoofing in, I flash by a modest Vilnius, a little
glossy art gallery café, with colorful hangings,
and
some great potato-kugal awash in oil.

Surrounded by breakfast at *Healthy Foods*, I slip back
into my forged Baltic skin; tight tabled to the brim only
one
Sunday per month, until I heard they'll close their curtains for good.

Now almost over and done, where Southside Chicago meets Lithuania,
that's my place, or was. Where Sox Park stays cold and closed a few
blocks
away, and where the waitress wears a gentle, humorless costume.

The family Biciunas will no longer perform. It's now my
last few winter Sundays there. The curtains are near-term,
and knifing downward for good.

My favorite Blynai with cheese and fresh fruit will be served on
South Halsted no more
by open
invitation.

The curtain calls are for Grazina Biciunas-Santoski,
a long standing order
and
a sullen ovation. I shall never taste her sweet Vilnius again.

DAN RYAN

Dan keeps going south
into another land,
and away from the
urban center.

Dan keeps going south
into another gate,
and away from the
city loop.

Dan keeps going south,
he keeps going south,
while everyone else
keeps pending in
for some hoop.

MR. CHICAGO

"Chicago is perhaps the most typically American place in America."
—James Bryce, 1888.

Some guys take their
          calls near the opera house,
the theater, or in a dive,
          and others by the green.

Their songs take a take stance
          toward the listener,
which for the better part,
          seems overt and plainly seen.

Songs not merely spelled out,
          but to be stage popular;
not to illustrate any kind
          of real fixed footing.

They entertain the given
          coterie, and loving it,
sing melodies mostly in
          target face of the listener.

And then there are other guys who
          make you swim to them,
and those who may enjoy
          to meet you in-between.

But this gentleman will
          hotfoot and crosswise the room,
so pleased to flatly take you,
          firmly by the neckband.

His affections were perchance
          picked-up in his days as a busker,
a whistling waiter, or as an old
          Midwest booster of a charting tune.

If he didn't make an impression,
      he didn't make a dime,
or if he didn't swagger, they
      knocked him right bolt down.

And so today you've come to
      hear his minor-key,
his ever up-tempo number,
      his lakeside tropic part.
His sound mostly leaning toward
      light melancholy, sometimes
passing through invisible joints
      of sorrow along the way.

And you've come to hear him even louder,
      by his firmness in melody,
if not, mostly by his modest
      catch-weed lyric.

Every hymn earshot as if
      not composed but mimed, his
words: "a big hometown"
      often collapse in tonal ambiguity.

The man just can't help it, his
      talents will not explain the force
which led an immigrant from station
      meagerness to wealth and renown.

And so his music keeps on living, a glint
      for each of his resident's hopes,
And this persists to sustain him, a mettle of
      neighborhood cultures.

And so he keeps playing on and on and on,
      with purely American notes.

ANDERSONVILLE

Once a chilly suburb,
  faraway from the
  flames of 1871,

There were no wooden
  houses in Chicago,
  so who could
  build and come?

But east of Clark with north
  to Foster, alien Swedes
  collected, and came to
  build and fix,

They proffered to make a life
  from forest wood,
  not holding the luxury
  of stones or bricks.

Alighting a nearby cherry orchard,
  building up their
  businesses, with two new
  blossoming streets.

Now they shoot a line of quality
  shoe and hardware stores,
  sundry restaurants and
  novel, local bakery beats.

It's become a flaming neighborhood
  at last, and just keeps smoking
  upward, but now in daring,
  newer, further sorts of ways,

The orchard Swedes now welcome
          other immigrants, Middle Eastern
          eateries; more *alien* peoples:
          like lesbians, cross dressers,
          and gays.

It's the model of a modern urban
          neighborhood, now it smolders,
          keeping the growing flame, unsparked
          by it's far away wooden, early days.

TOWERING THE INFO COMMONS AT LOYOLA

You
can be
still here,
relax, and surround
the daring beach high
up from the information
spyglass of the clever Jesuits.
Awake, you can see readers divinely
go for a dip before a portioning crosswise
spirit meets them from the slopes across the lake. Where
Old Marquette starts to chat. High up over there, students spin
you can read aloud the other letters in the library stacked high up
over here, on the other university face of the great Michigan sea. And,
how the hankering of their toppled books can verily channel a new joke
shift, while everyone's sleeping. They'll say it's where the troubles of a GPA
make today's cafeteria grub seem far more mediocre to any fare you might notice
in the watering holes of Rogers Park. Or the way your mom used to frame her food,
way back, before we all took on the gainsay of a real big Lakeside-Jesuit-study-firm.
Its about a college degree in all the immortal questions way, way up here. Which in just
four swift years will peripatetically soon encircle: the paying of taxes, the birthing of new kin,
a need for a caliber preschool; and then a little grousing about condo assessments or putting out
the cat twice daily. Those wide windows lofty up at the information commons proffer you an unearthly
rank, a tall glassy refuge where the soul can visit the lake—*thrust forward*. A Jesuit spyglass, with letters,
learning, and some first-class-sleeping above a lap top or a nearby fallen blackberry: *doze&study@luc.edu.*

ELEGY FOR MRS. O'LEARY

(In honor of Rose Auslander's *My Nightingale*.)

She was an artless missy by some other   clock.
Her gothic clover   eyes

And her fairness pull me   through
to this very   instant.

On my lake balcony she alights, one   peeper
an angel and the other a   fiend,

her very rivet a   *cow.*
When I spoke to her one warm   night,

her words to me where in gull.   Today
a shore bird romping the   beach

along Rogers Park. Every third   night
I hear her on my terrace by my   moon.

She bemoans the loss of   structures
She sings of long ago   Chicago.

Speaking of the flat roads of   Cook
County, as she preserves her   chants

and cradle songs only on those   singular
nights, almost near my very   seat

across from my table. She sits and carols   on
the balcony of   my urban   cell.

Second.

Subway Series

*"The rivalry is intense, but this is minor-league baseball.
It's supposed to be fun."*
—Tim Bawmann

PRIOR TO INDEPENDENCE DAY

Agone,
like barber's poles,
State Street pennant jacks
tatter bolt down from every
vaulting perch
higher up.

Agone,
Field's bags mixing
among the flowers and leaves, seem no
longer snagged and checked
in morning
traffic.

Agone.
Along State, July-the-3rd
remains a dismal siege. Yellow curbs
break into four colors: flame red, clean stripped
on snowy bands of white, with Macy's golden
pentacles among the
summer green.

Agone.
But for many, they bind our city banner:
offering four sad stars, gloomier white,
against two stripes of
darker, lamenting-river
blues.

Agone.
A loyal Midwest monument:
a singular ransom retail, on that great Street,
no longer salutes the saintly-hearted. All faithful
Chi-town shoppers have been entombed.

Agone.
A holy landmark, possessed by an imp and fiend supplier,
binds one and all: cries, jolts, and sneers offer louder threats: *"We will rise up,*
we will not buy, we will not spend . . . only Field's . . . and by no other name."

Begone!
Then, in a flash rising: free from all snare, each pennant waves four high ruby stars,
with three Christened whites, and two virgin blues. Welcoming the redeemed—losing all
the loyal doom.
It's now a brighter third morn: July the 5th! A holy half-price liberty. We forgive and we
consume.

TOURISTS

1. Like each and every one
       of us, they were in good cause,
visiting members to Capone's

lodge, holding
       nothing but what may be
inclined to bordering,

whatever law-breaking
       move they could have
saved. Not teensy frightened
       by the bird-man, Sing-Sing

or any state jug, they simply
       traveled here with fancies
once bred
       for city thugs.

2. Between light
       and bittersweet
dark: our famed
       pecking order
gave them a real

       dread and anxious
holiday here. All those
       Valentines, red massacres,
Cupid's cards and

       candies. And all our
pastries well-nigh, came to
       them duly pardoned
and Hollywood
       baked.

3. Virtues, sometimes make
       for disappointed tourists.
Absorbing sprinkled facts
       about magnificent miles,

they are forced to freeze off their
       picture palace hopes and then be
silent with us. Muted speaking of gassed
       tycoons, patron nobility or worse
yet, anything about Bugsy's mob.
       Our guests are put about to look for
better days and weeks of upright local
       boost, leaving out any or all tabloid

breezes. Banned. All gagster lore. Leaving
       them without Biograph bullets or thickening
big boss fog, they must order their donuts
       here quite warmed by a Springfield oven.

Then sometimes by a nearby precinct, or fixed
       and rubbery with filling frosted from good
ol' city hall. Sanitizing Chi-town's past
       only wings it toward gravitational

kitsch, or like the generic strip plazas
       of Iowa, Indiana and Wisconsin,
or worse yet, a maximum prison mall,
       one for all America, and holy
guarded in Twin-cities Minnesota.

LAND ON THE BEACH

Rhythmic
blowing of the
windiness,

Should
assure us just where
we are,

An
outstrip from its
halt to us

For
urban floating
is not far.

If poli-sci be
a selfish cry

Chicago
should not
understand.

When
she gusts it blows
for us,

We
live on filled-in
sand; and

For
what we now resist
to hear

We

soon make
no amends

If this be fact of living here
a coastal third of life depends

AT THE CASCADE

The late-summer sun had overruled,
      then, quietly sank before the giant screen.

It's shadows staring down, downward on the parking
      tarmac, only for Marisol to brush Josue daring

Him to witness how two Boys Town lads were kissing,
      in frame of their rear-view mirror.

Those boys had rock-bottom all the clothes they had
      against a hot August eve in West Chicago.

Sandra Dee and all their gang had just moved there,
      shortly after all the new window speakers

were tightly installed; so in a quick flash:
      "you're the one that I want"

would then alter everything about true, locked lovers. Forcing
      the lubricants in their hair to addle, and the popcorn,

hotdogs, and vanilla malts to shake and quake
      a new order of taste, setting their drive-in snuggling anew.

Suddenly it's not the fifties anymore, and the bolder truths of
      Ancient Grease will forever leap on and off all Hollywood scenes.

JAZZY-BLUE MYTH(S)

Every day is windy here and up
clear   of the goddess Ceres off
La Salle,

which will then swirl stability of
our   natural Irish-green
river.

It's true many gangsters still
romp   the loop and city
streets,

as Michael Jordan reigns the
sole   first fame,
before

and after wiped-out
Mr.   Al Capone;
and   the only

quiet calm is in the
toxic   free suburbs.
Whereas

ten-thousand to one love the Cubbie
losers   and
revile   the White Sox
Champs.

Cults of Oprah, Bob Newhart,
and   Donahue sponsor broadcast
re-runs

thrice daily; as the bitter gall for
NYC   wrecks our breed and need
to *invent.*

And *yes*, our first black president
is   really a trained Chicago-boss
machine,

and every punctual path on the CTA
makes   Benito Mussolini, quite
content.

SUBWAY SERIES

Their batting positions
Ever keen for a
Fray.
Their will, always ready

For strife about
Some way to parse
A swept series.

One higher than Madison,
The other, prouder below.

Both sand the water's edge.
Banished from the west,
They have no eastern
Territory on the compass.

Why such a
A stir about the
Zone?

Why such
A bout about the
Stakes?

The rest of Lincoln's log
Seems careless; and
There's truly no
bona fide debate:

Indifference to the
Little leagues
Topples no real
Springfield, shout.

But indifference
Makes confederate
Difference,

In Chi-town's
border between
North and south.

OCTOBER 31ST 2008, o.b.m

Aleph.

This morning Studs hoofed-path over to
The other loop,

Or the loop just walked to work this time
By him.

And both sides were all athirst, drinking
Pail by pail.

All heard his honest ledger with his valet's words,
Key by key.

And all scented his sound, his vernacular dictions,
Whiff by sniff.

They choose to hear him offer a few final
Every day reflections,

Picking out from him some stripped-down
Working class demands.

Granting him an office cubicle to surprise and
Illuminate, and then

More generous space marked to embrace the overlooked
And the ignored.

Beth.

But now this 31st, lifted masks,
Disguises and darken sidewalk lamps can never foot by ol' Studs again.

For they have interred him, perpetual
Amidst all these very Chicago souls—unembellished.

Beyond every Hallow's eve it was they
Who never costumed; and he never offered them a trick.

It was he who seldom reveled
With any barbaric holiday, or kitschy hometown jaunt.

Gimel.

Poised Broadcasters,
Scholars, Scribes,
Journalists, Philosophers,
Folklorists, Interviewers,

And Those Resisting
Any Hell-Raisers,
Keep Yourselves
Afar And, Aloof.

Only Those Bent
On Naked Masquerade
May Dare To Walk Over
Here Now, And Never

Beg For Treats, For
This Little Loop Won't
Greet You Upon Arrival.
It's Modest Space Can't
Welcome You All.

Double-Barreled Terkel
Has Got You Covered,
And The Wellborn
Haunt Is His Alone.

SHY TOWN

Never will you fake fine art,
On the trims of Navy Pier.

Never will you scab the Wrigley line,
For cold and pricey beer.

Never will you consume the salted sea,
By supplanting fresher beaches, nearer to flaxen Lunt.

Never will you find the fear to be second,
Or vim and hunger, ever for the front.

Never will a tall great Empire
Challenge that of a glossy, glassy Vies.

Never will you find a condo, or an office
On the lakefront, since they've imbedded the trees.

Never will you hear or see a symphony
So Elysian, or challenging to grapple.

Never will you find a little wish in these
Midwestern parts, to be a grand big apple.

NEW SPERTUS LIGHT

There's an older academic sleeve here and
      Some faithful facility for research,

A lecture series, a couple of workshops,
      And some cherish for museum exhibits.

But now, new transparent windows form 726
      Portals for one splendid illumination,

Combining 556 shapes and sizes which hasten the whole into
      An effect of deuce-ace amplitude, all

Forcing an even louder "yehi" which bellows out
      Along a fussy magnificent mile, which

Makes the surrounding desire to study from
      A newer *"shema"* all more sonic than before.

A fresh kosher café to the eye now tells you there's
      Even a better balance between

Windy city architecture, Torah
      And the Hebrew motive to enkindle.

And so here lies yet a better tonality to
      Jewish identity.

One which enfolds the immemorial
      Yet challenges the past perfect,

Newer, and unafraid of humanities'
      Best friend snapping a pair of

Wide-rimmed spectacles while keeping
      Company to the star of King David.

Along a pristine wall you'll find a winsome hound, a single star and
        Ten thousand sticks of light
                Now serving to froth the Michigan horizon.

A winsome hound, a single star and
        Ten thousand sticks of light serving
                To scrape the south sky Loop.

TEN VERSES AT THE JOFFREY MATINEE

"I would believe only in a God that knows how to dance."
—Friedrich Nietzsche

V1. On any afternoon you can bet
on a vibrant service, sitting the hours out
within a cavern wall

of Mr. Sullivan, watching ignited upswings,
and the ghost of airy Mr. Arpino,

peeping brassy from his box.

V2. In your raked seat up, up beyond the vetch,
you can view how butterflies land and snakes rattle,

how Chicago flies.

V3. You can witness how they navigate delicate
nuances, and in which way each reign of Terpsichore

is defiantly profaned.

V4. Publishing your eyes on dances with
violations, melting awe with your heart against an

often canned symphony.

V5 A jockeying *pas de deux,* flat vestments
unclothed, jagged and resentful. Your afternoon

can quickly swim into yummy holiness.

V6. Ballet can be so complicated,
so refined, so brand-new; then frame

itself with incense and chromatic gauche.

V7. High up, Hades and Eden are everyplace,
so grueling to be pious, you don't know what any

kind of really good prophesy means.

V8. So you quickly travel up your hands to the
communion table; and let it be flashily known
that you are now quite very full.

V9. You can't side with the hallowed hymns, or
even the sober rites, since only the gods have any

honest good sense in these kinds of matters.

V10. Your Sunday afternoon only fathoms obscurity,
and slips away from any sound, fit doctrine. You've been to the Joffrey,

and just received a really, really good dose of religion.

HALSTED BUS

COME you cartoonists,
hang on a strap with me here
at seven o'clock in the morning
on a Halsted street car.
—Carl Sandburg, *Halsted Street Car*

Hopping on haggles
        to be an endless piazza
of outlets, restaurants,
        banks and even a chip or two
of . . . distinctive emporia.

Riding too long on this
        pullet seems to bring
granular retention of fruit
        markets, old Maxwell
merchandise, and a few migrants
        shouting
for . . . a ransom.

As number eight passes
        over many more streets, and
steers her way down toward the
        stockyards, her open windows
filter whiffs of a Polish, chili-cheese fries
        and then a glimpse
of . . . Italian ice.

Since her former bell's departed from ringing,
          her recorded chime echoes in position
now. Some days her fresh hydraulic elevates a
          wheelchair happy-up, then down to
the pavement, as she offers a Viet Nam
          vet a sample of a bustling
coop . . . that day.

Number eight covers the whole; and all the
          assorted spot her unexpected arrivals.
Sometimes three of her flocked back to back,

as rancor builds and a trinity of lady
          drivers strive to point away from cackle
and . . . blockade.

          Then all appears frozen, as side-walkers and
bikers pass her by mostly two or three
          yellow-lights to red-lights and countless, faltering
stops to . . . halts.

          Number eight's all her very own egg in the pocket.
She's her own Halsted-hauler. Up, up to
          Broadway and back, she's
the main . . . liner.

She captures all readers, callers, last-puff smokers,
          and those creating their text, as she carts
north towards south. And then she clutches
          south towards north
all over . . . again.

She's poultry every senior respects.
      Most visitors need of necessity.
She's ticker, mortal and lifeline
      to the pupils of DePaul and UIC.
She's a rider home to the homeless,
      and a bringer to the pubs of Lincoln Park.
She's a cart to five blues bars and the Kingston Mines, as
      she passes maybe four, five or even six Walgreen's.
She's no seven, nine or even an arrant ten,
      she's the number *eight* and she's our township hen.

CLAVERING THE BEAN

Possessing so bright a reflection, so brilliant
    a likeness of the millennium archway

Before my eyes, I pointed myself out
    to me; then flitted, waggled and fluttered.

At *cloudgate* all observation is improved, and surface
    pleasures open all subtlety to deeper forms of thought:

To butterfly strokes, intemperate insects, carnassial monkeys; and
    then, the occasional flash of a disposable Kodak.

The tendency to liken myself to fun house standard does not
    harrow my modest reputation.

All of my esthetic now seen and felt and heard by others,
    I know it's safe to be goofy, playful and quite unripe.

Disadvantaged so long of childhood memories, I have a new
    close by distortion, and abandon my office cubicle catty corner the park.

My wispy need for expression becomes quite fit, and worth
    more than three months of therapy or twenty self-help books.

How disadvantaged I am; and how underpaid for such corporate
    bondage, and yet more mellow earnings for joy so deep,
    so curing and soothing to the self, can be seen not far away from my office

Found over here at the bean, in the winter airs of Millennium Park,
    where the toddler's bird bath is dry, and thirty trees are now bald;

Where sightseers research the seemingly infinite visual thrills
    and mysteries which are waiting to be given away by pure childish fun.

NORTHWESTERN POLAR BEARS

"If you stand still there is only one
way to go, and that's backwards."
—Peter Shilton

Into our stubborn heads there reasons
A nearby beach, a petty shore where twelve jocks

Set out, peeled and power-nude,
Just before dawn, in frigid, frigid rectitude:

Toward that place, with no torch, locker or sky
Hiding the melted glacier, from our frozen college sand.

Early dawn, plum and thin as lace, so fraternal
In its daring pace, we chose to begin our frosty loom.

First: Wildcat towels, placed purple on the rocks.
Then swiftly, we scoop the lake between our crotch.

Raiding the waters, we then carry our quest
First down, down then up, toward a budding Evanston sky.

Shore fishes twitch us, quick and stark;
In our goading zone, they nab, and nab our mark.

We chortle: *Come Polar Bear with Us!* as
Our beat rises full throttle: and we sink into the polar coast.

Our knees and toes will drink Lake Michigan as
Ice cubes ruffle into every fleshy and stiff male fissure.

On that day we meet our tarn, and winter all over again.
Twenty-four balls, and the frigid, frigid Northwestern shore.

Together we call out, to our gentle growing sun:
We'll be back, we'll be back again. Next year, for more!

GWENDOLYN BY THE LAKE

(a tribute to *We Real Cool* by Gwendolyn Brooks)

Roosevelt University Musicians
Seven at the Lakefront

We real cool. We
love school. We

Play late. We
Strike straight. We

Lute life. We
drop strife. We

Jazz June. We
Watch moon.

THE SOUTH SIDE BALLPARK

(1st tribute to *The Red Wheel Barrow* by William Carlos Williams)

so much depends
upon

a champion
ball park

plagued with empty
bleachers

outside the packed
ale houses

Third.

On Behalf of Lovable Losers

"Chicago Cubs fans are ninety percent scar tissue"
—George F. Will

THE ASHEN PUMP HOUSE

(2nd tribute to *The Red Wheel Barrow* by William Carlos Williams)

so much depends
upon

an ashen pump
house

glazed with zebra
clams

inside the sky blue
lake

SOUTH SIDE PABULUM

Soft diets and
Jenny Craig
clearly can't
squelch those
unannounced and
quickened
      queasy, queasy quests

for Chicago
finger food, and
them sausage and
peppers with red
love apples
on your
      deep, deep dish pizza.

Nor the livid
lust for lemon
ice, left over and
lingering
near Taylor
Street for such a
      short, short sultry season.

Nor the red hots
with celery seeds on top,
snubbing any sensation
of catsup or any
bits of out of line
relinquish for
      sweet, sweet raw relish.

Nor the garish
queues for garnished
Garrett's popcorn with
gleaming gobs of
fruitless caramel, and
three gustoes of
      cheddar, cheddar cheese.

Nor the un-pickled
Polish poking its
mustard side with cross-town
Cubbie fans waiting outside
The Cell, for possibly
an unlikely win of a
      gone, gone given game.

Nor the Italian beef
belching its way
into a seemingly
soundless stroll past
Maxwell Street, then
calling and seducing every
starving Sox fan strolling on by.

In Chi-boodle there's Gold Coast cuisine and of course
      many four and five star stables.

There's goody grub near any canny curb in Lakeview,
      then it's duly doled at Wicker Park and Lincoln tables.

There's drowning drink and there's always
      giddier garb at all the winning Wrigley hops.

There's Addison scrutiny and surveillance, while begging tickets; even
      shouting and shambling da-scalpers, which often welcomes da cops.

But surely enough, you can sensuously seek
                    your relished red, red hot,
                        your deep, deep dish
                            your un-pickled Polish or
                                your boastful Italian beef,

                                And for the better part by foot, stroll
                                up and down, many a South Side street.

STREETWALL RIME

Our facades are lawful and essential,
        But so is the whole kinship
        Of lakefront horizon conjoint,

One which would intensify and clutter
        The skyline, could set a terrible
        Case in point. Should we license

One monstrous building growing up,
        Then our agreed Streetwall
        Will be blotted out. If only one

Zigzags up again, and boasts with a
        colossal rise, we're finished
        Far shorter than stout.

Twelve blocks of building must always run
        from Randolph to Eleventh, and next
        Confront Millennium Park.

We let seventy-story constructs emerge,
        And we mend everything mindless
        From finish to start, and so

Should developmental pressures deplete
        This singular character, and
        Efface these worshipful places,

Our front door to the city welcomes
        America's finest and lost,
        Of historical spaces.

OUTSIDE BAHAI TEMPLE

later on
at the temple,
you came out
smelling like
a tinted rose.

there was an
air of the Taj
Mahal.

and the
scent of
Baha'u'llah
on your breath.

they gave you
the best gifts
and the best
words in their
quiet, and

you gave off
the freshness
of permission
to be unblocked
without doctrine
or opinion.

you helped me see how
a junior prophet loved
your moments
of glad grace,

how a great white
temple had arms
with no end
and no beginning,

then you helped me
meet heaven, light rain
and everything
poised us toward
renewal.

ON BEHALF OF
LOVABLE LOSERS

the prowess of losing is a fine art
      and very, very easy to subdue
            we loose something every day
                 but we never love losing our cool
                     we rather wish for winning
                         we want to win and want it most
                             it raises us high and favors the self
                                it gives us the power to boast.

    we loose sleep
    we loose time
    we loose money
    we loose prime
    we loose lotteries
    we loose pounds
    we loose hope
    we loose ground

    we loose virginity
    we loose graces
    we loose salvation
    we loose races

But.......does anyone really,
                truly,
                  honestly
              really love
           losing the WORLD SERIES for over one

harmful,
hostile,
bruising,
hurtful
CENTURY?

One Should Think . . . . *Not!*

GREEN MILL COCKTAIL LOUNGE

The place I go to find myself is not
so far away. Against a corner on the path of a
Lawrence Street jalopy.

Non-smokey eyes behold the brassy
beauty that surrounds the crowdedness, and the
struggle for just one little throbbing set.

Refreshing, renewing, a fragrance in my ears that somehow
flags on my iPod shuffle. If I had a magic megaphone
I would open the door and just crank it up.

Riffs and sets swimmingly smile in the face of stormy
Uptown weather, as a scholar or two risks
smoking them 'ciggies' outside.

Inside we can weep for joy together. Smile in the
face of a stormier upwind and wonder who just might
now come in with a fresh new horn.

I can say the gods are good to bridge former gangsters
and the condo developers next door. To leave them both
in the earshot of some jazzy paradise.

When your there you don't know your looking for the hidden,
searching for the notes once carved by sons of slaves, now played by a few
pale college chums or a grand ivory Wicker Park scat.

The power of the light-green grind cocktail lounge is not your fault.
The force is theirs. When the wailing is all over, departing silence
welcomes all the required answers.

The Green Mill you see is really not green at all. Its walls and floor
are haunted by the many souls of shoes and struts of Jim Crow runaways.

The mill is really ebony, and her heritage can never be taken away
     by anything less than the brightly emerald—black soul!

C.S.O.

A
powerful
precision instrument
that plays even chandelier
works with an uncommon
pliancy, and an unforeseen
beauty; which flirts with
movie scores and reasons the
kind of excitement which espouses
illuminated sabers and stilettos.
Euphony that howls and roars and
drags you through a dark night of
the soul; then lays you down up again
for layover and recline
in manners which enkindle
philharmonic *invidia.*
Rolling thunder from the percussion sires
a menacing mixture of hard driven
strings, and woodwind figurines, which when
heard must be jubilant, bittersweet and
passing always for absolute crystal.
Boulez still breaks his back with his
bare hands for sensibility, gloss and touches
of operant word painting.
Ever convincing, his line drawings figure to
be cinematic short subjects to gentler
more introverted moments in misty shifts of text.
Lurking movement bounces, inverted dotted
rhythms, and seductive syncopation pushes
and yet remains a singular and fantastical identity.
Rendering individualities between western
Europe and South Michigan Avenue,
poets leisurely run out of adverbs and
adjectives to demurely describe
our united family of
notes shifting all cycles
from A above
middle
C.

THE PALLID PIER

1

NEAR the loop east is blue,
downhill is all
strip air,
and downstairs at the famous
towers there sleeps none.

Steering along the river,
below
the Tribune beat,
there's an eye for frowsy
gallery calls, and
a broadcast window

Which sanctions verandas
and buses
a trip
a lovely
gimcrack boulevard.

Learned visitors will truckle further
along the bank, and seek the
freshen benches there, to stop, fob
and
watch a great architectural prize.

Finding a reward unrivaled,
a place for rest, a visual
hush, a museum treat, right
there and
all
for free!

25

They seem to know best by
watching modern sky art
placed
on Delphic pedestals,

With cruisers
chanting the greenish river as it
meets the nearby bluish
and
fresher sea.

2
AWAY from Merchant,
Mart and passing by and
by
from the trance of
the sculptures and their sacred span:

Too many more will spot a heavy
hamburger wheel,
a trickster of lies and for fries
will gladly pay
a hamburgler's fee.

Over there: it's novelty bears
with sox and bulls with
hawks,
the navy dock
is all but kitsch. With names of ships,

And edible quips, it offers a breezy
post at best
to stump, waste your change
and then
to
come and pee.

The mettle of sponsors
and the
over-pricing of beer look to offer
something altogether
uniform with

Every mid-west mall,
and south-burb plaza,
or the "taste"
with
all its stalls.

And yet they
seem to
to leave behind
my
Parthenon?

4.
WHY do they come in droves,
and travel up in vain,
and choose to pass a visual wonder,

Catching the wheel
and leaving behind the river
and
the pedestals of modern antiquity?

For what, to—look?, to: smell?
to: hear?, to buy,?
to—*tell?*

They come visit a
wind glorious city,
to arrive
and
not absorb the scene?

Simply deflecting a so vernacular
and majestic
address and with such a
dreadful, dreadful aim;

They crave a compass buying
position
to quiet,
and quash,
the fresh marbles scraping our skies.

The pallid pier's their very first
Chicago post,
as it
brushes a quiz never
on
the actual tourist map.

Not spotting the prank question
visitors will come
and answer to a mall, leaving behind
the
River's outdoor museum peak.

HOMELAND COLORS

City banner waves a top second,
Against a taller, flattering Ol'
Glory. She beckons every up and about
Pole, jetted-out and in full face of the sun.

City banner welcomes the noonday rays by her *four**** stars, two blue stripes==and a three-white-setting.*
She too, forges a fluttering
Fathom with every gusty wind, near Daley Plaza.
Pigeons and lake doves she troubles by her public racket.

Two powder blue river twigs sway amid
Four clarets: six-point stars. By a familiar draft,
She marks all things sharper by her soft
Imprimatur, then soars boldly downhill
The lengths of doors, with every tough patrol car shield.

When she charges the evening moon, with her *four**** stars, two blue stripes==and a three-white-setting;*
City banner then spawns a daintier beckoning.
By her nightly limelight she holds like a
Sporting starlet receiving her four red
Carpet clusters for the very first time.

For she too, is red, white and blue, minus
Eight stripes and, forty-six stars all
Crowed in her upper left hand, but still her
Fabric flutters high; her daily toast to the
City no less united, majestic or grand.

MATCHLESS DINING

Supping Chicago requires a
reverse
slant critique,
Menus gauged not from the cap
down,
but from the fathom, uphill.

Sensible and even
perk up
choices at every grade, so
Bottom
dwellers can grab a hold and gorge.

Here you savor, feel welcomed
and not
just tolerated.
Value item prices always
grace the
nature and identity of this big town.

Elsewhere more pricey fare will
be fattened
with tariffs, but here, lower end is
prime
opportunity for expression.

Govern from the very bottom
of the list,
and you can get
ambitious.

It's tops too if your limousine requires
cuisine,
in need of a *Cros Parantoux*
or a star
grilled *dorade royale.*

We're not only here about gimcrack food
by any
means, just unmatchable values;
and peerless
taste at any price.

Just good, sweet home Chicago cookin'.

BUCKINGHAM HIBERNAL

The fountain
        is covered, now
and the tourists are all sitting
        at home elsewhere;

And my girlfriend
        and me are left once
more, frozen and watching
        all alone.

No paper cups on
        the gravel, broken
balloon strings or nickels in
        the water.

No melted ice cream cones
        on the fence, no little girl
gauging tantrums against
        her daddy.

This chiliad fountain is very, very
        quiet; all the pigeons
and squirrels have even traveled astray
        and left.

As for the students who worked
        or even tried to clean
here, all the big summer spending
        is gone,

And all good odds are lost
        for nipping
some foamy cold, cold
        underage beer.

Only compassionate weather
          spawns this jet-spring alive,
until we can finally serve and clean it
          up again.

For those who love to pass, or even
          marvel here, our majestic
fountain by the lake remains silent
          and muffled,
Until the next great Chicago summer
          will appear, if and when it
arrives again. Until then, winter is here
          for good.

PICASSO AT DAWN

I approach Daley plaza
And quietly pose in utter secrecy.
Sunlight arrives in full vacancy
While every flagpole is abiding
                  at
                      nude
                          mast.

I stand on my toes of miniature
Grandeur and watch a giant baboon
Woman lose her color and
Some of her power for a
                few more, clever . . . seconds.

As my shadowy figure looms greater
Than her sizable metal figure.
I have some power for a
                few more, clever . . . seconds

Strange lady baboon holds back
Her smile like Da Vinci's *Mona
Lisa*, only this time she's a bit smaller
&   I
    am
      clearly
        MAMMOTH.

Soon the rising sun will make her splendor
Clear again, and my stature will be sober,
And the great pedestal of Pablo will once
Again be the rusty running board for city
children to chase and follow each other
                                    in
                      a
                         sunny
                                merriment

                                all
                                   their . . . clever own.

SEVEN HAIKU

7.

The chief asteroid belt
knows a city by the lake,
  and it blows windy.

6.

Between *Chiayi*
and *Chichibu* the one to
  love is: THREE, THREE, FOUR.

5.

Carbonaceous group
between Mars and Jupiter
  calls herself: "Hilda."

4.

Hilda *knows* quite well:
there's nothing like a rock named
  after Chicago.

3.

And every rock *knows*:
just windy cities are named
  after Hilda's home.

2.

There's also a loop,
on sister rock in the sky,
     grab the "EL" and go.

1.

See, visit and hear
this toddlin' galactic town,
     it's a free transfer.

FOUR SEASONAL TANKAS

I.
Winter hands and feet
drop near Millennium; in
fluid frost they tread

breaking the day's skating to
halt and glide to my surprise.

II.
Autumn hands and feet
drop near Millennium; in
fluid leaves they stand

breaking the eve's election to
halt and dance to my surprise.

III.
Summer hands and feet
drop by Millennium; in
fluid shorts they feed

breaking the noon's sunshine to
halt and taste to my surprise.

IV.
Springtime hands and feet
drop near Millennium; in
fluid crowds they come

breaking *Cloudgate's* mirror to
halt and muse to my surprise.

THAT CHOCOLATE SMELL

The orange-cloud burnt sky
     Tainted and boomed from the traffic,
     Still smells of confectionery chocolate.

Just around the corner somewhere close to Jackson
     And Monroe, every single nostril
     Sniffs the same old whiffs.

Hershey Park for one, another revives Russell Stover,
     While Emil J. Brach chases Miss Fannie May.
     And the traffic just continues and continues.

Passing through the windy city near the south loop,
     Commerce also passes and no nostril really
     Succeeds in being successful at any recovery.

One mark of chocolate may be as honorable as the next,
But then of course, it must give full dignity
To every other beak as it sees fit and offers best robust.

As for myself, there may be less saccharin for sure, but for daily visitors
     Perhaps a little more *procyanidin flavinoids,*
     And then a bit more chaste Nox cocoa.

Truth being told it's not sulfur, octane, or even volcanic ash.
     Who dare complain about the quantum? Who would
     Transpose gustier toxins from Mexico City, Tokyo or L.A.?

And so we must welcome those curls of chocolate which flavor the city
Next to Pilsen on their way down toward UIC; and the traces which may hide
And stick in the trees near Jane Addams Hull House.

And still later, wandering further to make a quick calm near that traffic light.
     You do admit you've smelled it near the
     Halsted and Maxwell intersection? We've heard your comments.

And so all you who call or pass-through, skipping by from other
       Provinces and states, may you gain infinite blessings when
       You too stop, grin, and think about the same nasal questions.

And so discover that your curious nostrils
       Are not bigheaded, but simply contented, unfolded,
       And quite cheerful. In truth: they've been sprinkled with cocoa.

Home.

Cross-Town lovers

*"Chicago will give you a chance,
the sporting spirit is the spirit of Chicago"
—Lincoln Steffens*

ENCOMIUM: HAROLD WASHINGTON LIBRARY

W.
      Majestic red brick, mantled
And trimmed in green,

      Witnesses a mayor's switch
To royal halls of city scene.

      Proving a moniker's proud
Strength and warrant fury,

      Displays a strong and braving figure,
A people's triumph, a black man's story.

      Bold not brittle, soft and bright,
A palace blend of all not white.

      It's silent mysterious, alluring roof
Watches us daily with promise and proof.

X.
But Washington's library fetches
forth a variety of dealings,

Causing some to frown,
and proffer harsher feelings,

As many more will smile,
borrow, and *read, read, read*

From its tightly shelved and
Blest annals among us.

Especially a growing,
Literate nation, integration

And rising, rising,
American justice.

Y.
Nothing more, a brick book
Reminder, and an ebony mayor

From Chicago. His bullying
Collection really brings us nothing

But musty printed books; bound and vault
Journals, and ample, ample metal shelves.

Only a fair city's municipal
Memory. It's really no actual menace,

Or any contest to our father George's
Beloved, and first foundational name.

You see Prince Harry really only wants
To quickly step aside, as some city dukes

Would have him do, and gladly leave
Behind his commanding, red book edifice.

Z.
Yes, Hal's really quite willing to pack his stately bags
And seize an even larger roof , a whiter residence,

He's all set to catalogue his many, many bedtime books
For the nation's first black commander of troops.

He's content to read and read his new chief quietly to sleep,
And every night, in a crowned, more efficient sort of way.

He's thrilled to lend a hand and help re-organize a president's desk.
Unseen, he rises up from Chicago, and now adorns an Oval Office.

THIRD COAST WINTERS

(For Dr. Arlene Swartzman)

"I miss everything about Chicago, except January and February."
—Gary Cole

I.
Why should Mr. Hibernal
carry on as he does? Why
don't we just open
the door and give him
his hideous
haggard hat? Why do residents take-on
                                        to
                                        keep dwelling here? When we don't wish to seem
                                        frigid

                                                        on
                                                        the Paulina platform?

Why are things so peculiar by this inland coast? Why do one, and nearly all, really
                                                        desire a smoother
                                                        warmer,
                                                        whipping
                                                        in
                                                        the end?

Why will iciness ever finger so formidably bloated, when we really covet a calmer winter;
and not squat factors   of
                                                        Chiding, blazing frost?

Why are there no outside cafes, open-air along our February coastal edge? When we really
crave some qualification for building a wall-free, wrap-around coffee bean banking? Like
you'll unearth in maybe   Miami or
                                                                San
                                                        Fran?

Why do we feel so *needy* breathing on a freshwater ice cube?

Why does all this keep happening to us? Why will our tolerance for atmospheric
                                        torture not lose any
                                        real arctic,
                                        fresh frontier?

Why, won't even seven days of winter light, never dissolve the blackened snowstorm
dung?

Why do we even dare to commune with a dreadful witless,
                                        dark and bitter winter?

II.
Because we understand the sun will once again
        be tender, early and yellow.
Because we discern the clocks will once again
        be so pleased, and shift to DST.
Because we realize once more how
        fireworks will erupt every weekend by Navy Pier.
Because we know how a grand
        Symphony will voice once more on our front lawn; no longer in the frozen hall.
Because we deem again the
        boats will exit their bulge, from the docks at Belmont Harbor.
Because we know for certain: the shrubs, the florets and every tree
        will license back their bright foliage and their sweet enduring scent.

III.
Or is it in truth, because we
Remember the roaring sounds
Of
Baseball games: *al fresco?*

Or the cheer after cheers which
Resonate from the roof-top bleachers
Adjacent Wrigley Field, then echo back awake, from the upper decks
Atop the
South Side Cell: *pied-a-terre?*

IV.

Such easy grounds: the fantasies of this our living city summer paradise,
which will quickly
muster
Mr.
Hibernal's lifeless door with goddess Pomona: *coup-de-grace,*

Then swiftly dupe our
images of a burning urban hell,
reminding us of our
duty to
resolve all our judgment here and settle: "*Urbs in horto*"

ZEBRA LOUNGE

A.
In another era,
prohibition died
and an
infant banded
buck was
born,

Abloom—a tiny
tiny piano bar,
and
fed, and fed with
garish
zebra-papered
memorabilia.

He's tucked inside
and between the ghosts
of
some courtly Chicago
brownstones.

He still poses neatly
titled night caps,
while his baby drags
are
calmed with
hard-core
rum and Coke.

He kicks a romp
about roster
of
keyboard standards,
and
chesty dry

martinis to live for.

Z.

Shout him quirky,
kinky far-out
and
even kitschy today,

But the baby
zebra
keeps
holding back
no one,
he's now
a legal gem.

Such an old
and
trusty keeper
of the bootlegger,
and sly, sly
moon shiner;

But they say he
still haunts
every soaker
he's
ever
exonerated.

And he
outlives
every cheery
toper endorsing his
birthday:

December 5th, 1933.

MONTROSE MORNINGS

Birth of dawn,
Brings a few shafts of fair haze,
     breaking the pitch.

As displays of
White sails leave the harbor,
     gulls cry wide and full.

Morning begins.
Loading the dark-skinned sky,
     glittering sparkles reveal
     all starboard faces.

A fresh chance for
Another voyage,
     stalks another weekend,
     almost ended.

As death of October
Quietly threatens a few remaining
     days of breaking pitch,

Shorter ones start rolling down at
Chancy speed, and every
     sail will soon descend and

Cover-tight, every swollen head of hair.

Along with distant shadows,
Waiting November chases every
     Rainbow, Brown and Chinook,

With the first rush of waiting winter.

It pushes bottom traffic from the wet
    World below, calling all salmon,
    and trout, to take warmer cover.

Then, birth of dawn
Brings a few shafts of fair haze,
    breaking the pitch,

With fins of floating ice.

SUMMER'S U of C SEMINAR

(For Prof. Vincent Samar, philosopher king)

Estival. Festival. *Lawn.*

Take good notes: it's the mow
Down philosophy for all
Wisdom and festivity . . .

Deduce everything hands down,
With confidence; then carry out your proof
On the Hollywood sand . . .

Skill quicker logic, with
Gruffer time, abandon all needless chores;
And lurch all farm duties . . .

Common sense is no longer fair game.

Filch gelato breaks. Pilfer *Ping Pong*
Chop stick takes, and pay a far, lesser wage,
To the punching of your clock . . .

Estival. Festival. *Pawn.*

Build lucrative chat, amid chance
Diversions and Boyz Town coffee, which should
Always necessitate toward infinity . . .

Mandatory calls are not
Real numbers, forget the proof:
Leave it to Dunford and Schwartz . . .

Biking must inform all your propositions.
Always dine *al fresco,*
And you'll keep a valid claim.

Poise syllogisms preset: then tangent
Your reading list with scholarly writ by lighter
Tunes, singing from your iPhone pal . . .

You must always savor the warm and
Bright Chicago days reasonably,
Their constant is simply
Too variable and their seconds, restricted . . .

Estival. Festival, *Gone.*

CROSS-TOWN LOVERS

We can look
like love bees
another
time.

Let's buzz in
tandem pair
along
Sheffield

and pollinate by
the lake in
separate dugouts
for now.

We can always
thicket again
later; away from
those dividing
beaches.

After tasting pollen
first at your bench,
and then the next
at mine.

After cheering
some baseball
in city wide
swarming,

and yielding a
sting or two
in married,
metropolis
fun.

Then later we can
make honey together
back at our
own quiet
suburban comb.

NO REGRETS: A POST-MODERN MASSACRED VALENTINE

"I adore Chicago. It's the pulse of America."
—Sarah Bernhardt,

{**P**lease Mr. Aldermen let's just not **a l t e r:**}

^^^**Or well be…. so hidden or** *r e p e n t a n t about*
"Scarface"…**C A P O N E**
Or   them purchased C i c e r o
Cops or the memory of   that good old holy man *B i l l y   S u n d a y*
Or that red box-of-candy m a s s a c r e
Or even so afraid to point>>> to>>> a l l those
Untouchable gangster images or pay-tron $pay-offs$ or B I G boss
mayorzzz,
Or those too m a n y troubles: from Mr. D i l l e n g e r 's
Last stand at the now Victory Garden's BIOGRAPH,
Or t h a t polluting convention or Ol' *"Momo"* **GIANCANA**
Decades, and eons, eons ago! or by Mrs.
O' L e a r y 's   old cow's careless l o s t con*fusion*
or even the sullied *reprimands and maybe even happy housing*
Offered to craaaaazed Evanston-lady…hairy C a r r y Nation: and her
+*p r o h i b i t i o n e r s***+**

{*P*lease Mr. Aldermen let's just not **v e t o:**}

^^^and Well....be so happy to **v o t e** for the
Luster of Miss O p r a h, the QUEen of TalK,
Or "*M.J*"*., and h i s far, far too many*
Rings **or Jer-ry!, Jer-ry! or the** *Bull's Jerry too, or The "Kingston Mines"*
Or W G N nationwide, or SOX-Win 2005! and B.L.U.E.S. bars
Or H a r r y C a r a y's gig-gly glasses, or even *F e r r i s B u e l l e r,*
Or rough-tough R o y k o or the lofty
Stamp of S t u d s Terkel or to even stand on
Carl S a n d b e r g ' s BIG shoulders, or on the gift of the 1st black
prezzzzz,
Or even f o r that matter; TheBLuES Bros., or NeLson ALGREN & then...
Some r e a l, real good, Judy-CHICAGO
S u p p e r at a neat
Topside t a b l e way, way, way uP in
The H a n c o c k, (or the have you: the bruce—W i l l i s Towers)?
Or better yet, even swallow-up a pickle-top, celerey-seasoned
Hot dog (near the hiPPos or the FlamingOs) nearby the waters
Just in side, at the Lincoln Park zOO—oh, yes...the *FREE, Lincoln Park* **Z O O!**

{*P*lease Mr Aldermen...lets not alter, but let it go—it's true, it's true:}

My big-onion, smashing-pumpkin, sweet kind of big-shouldered, Toddlin'
town-on-the-make,
C H I C A G O.....................................is!

NO EAST ON THE COMPASS

There
ain't
no set east in this blues-town, so the
blocky
grid
compass dupes

only three views for a jazzy
and wincey west, and a choosy or so north side
amid the Wrigley
ball
park shrine.

Pointing is up, up real north, *up* . . .
just below Evanston graveyards right
smart aweigh
of
Rogers Park.

Pointing is down, down real south, *down* . . .
near the stockyards and resting on the
distant flats to
the
University of C.

Pointing is just over, over, *west* . . .
Just sunset toward Idaho and Iowa,
Over and beyond every land, maybe even
the
Pacific brim.

But they say there ain't no set, put *east* . . .
in this town, so our blocky compass neglects a point,
but everyone's clawing and fighting
to
settle

There though. It's just a splashy, wet, *wet* . . .
novel water joint neighborhood called
the
LAKE.

HOMETOWN SOUTH

Late at night you can't
separate the heed of home-town stead
from *da* Bears or *da* streets and *da* cops,

Or the echo of Ozzy,
sweeping thousands of souls at the
Soxer's 2005 World Series blow-out,

Near Sis Daley's place and
the monastery down the street. All around there's a tough
very distinct rough, black and white hominess.

And at times it's not cute like when boys are
holding hands along where North Halsted kisses
Broadway and the bars, or anywhere along Melrose & Aldine.

Those fresh flowers and trees along Dr. King's Drive
spill out everywhere sometimes looking a bit cross
from far too many air-tight Bridgeport Bungalows.

Under the great South Side starlight,
there's still some grounds for a bit of bad, bad Leroy Brown.
It sometimes fosters an air of gritty, poor neighborhood

Night vision, and causes for annoyance
while footing across 31st, and bumping into old pasty King Kong,
and then finding he's not smarter than a junk yard dog.

RECIPE FOR THEATRE HERE

*(inspired by Pablo Neruda and dedicated to
Richard Christiansen and Michael Egan)*

ALONG Chicago's
restless lake
lives a bright-hued
peacock,

a mounting bird
with feathers
like blueing snow.
HE'S everywhere
along the city's brim,

and within the coast
where the zebra clam
was also born:
thick and rich,

a feathery talent
for the stage.
AS you enter his storefront
holding, for a curtain recipe,
you'll see a patched fabric

quilted clean like a
a tailored cover,
leaving the ample
drape by the lake:

open to the world;
and done with cutting edges.
YOU'LL smell the vivid
peacock

and how he spangles,

ready for a
hearing.
WHILE plucking out
your modest playbill

of salts and seasons,
you'll then hear his
fresh aroma,
while turning the pressed pages
of honking text
with Court
with Steppenwolf
with Victory Gardens
with Goodman and

at last, with Second City
until all that's send-up
turns to trickled stock.
MEANWHILE you must swiftly,
quickly steam those zebra clams,

until they fix,
so the juices
of the pages and
the fresher water
muscles

bind together.
THEN, gently
greet the grand
peacock
and let him slide into halo,

let him steep in the broth
of your hidden pot, to reduce
and marinate.
LATER

all that is quested:

a dashing of peeled Terkels
dropped into the deep
like a sandy oak swaying,
then to slowly stir,
until the salted meats of Mamet

are warmed into the broth,
and the flavors
of fried loop, onions, and Letts
rises to the top,
newly bound together,

SO that in this very public
work of our own cookery
you may come to
recognize the very yummy
of consommés and casseroles.

SUNDAY IN THE ART INSTITUTE

Among the benched halls,
A spreading perch of light,
From a blue Chagall, while

Windows work at
Angles only clergy
May congratulate.

See how many listen
To holy paintings
While sitting with

Padded Headphones,
Which bespeak a sacred
Visitor nearby touching that

Seurat found in their
Tourist account book.
Quiet, quiet in the wings,

Passing just up against
The wire roadblock not to
Startle the Artwork ushers.

Hushed in the institute, and
Just nigh a faith whisper.
Nice quiet pilgrims touching relics.

Seemingly they all seem to watch
Or hear just what they are looking
For, and no one seems to really care,
No one even passes a collection plate.

ALTA VISTA TERRACE

i.
THERE sits here a peg down
terrace, with exactly forty
front doors. A fair bend in
Lakeview just off of Mayfair,
On the London side of

the tracks. Here in sweet
Chicago, where the baby
mansions have mirrored bay
windows, and each single sleeps

no more than four by every
stop; where the colder lake
meets the English Atlantic,
in a common homey crop.

Seeming to blend all familiar
turn of the century ways;
a Midwestern wick, to
former English kingdom days.

This is our prairie tribute to
metropolitan anomalies, a kiss
among continental cousins, a
hidden tale of two cities.

Here a route built by the
geld Mr. Gross, holds regard
for all the showy, a world of
the former, thus branding
his every love for Bric-a-brac.

ii.

BUT the shapely ways of cousin
England, won't take deeper dwelling
ground, in our rougher—bluer towne.
There's no construction call for more
and more, royal tracks like this.

So Mr. Gross's style won't seem to root
or even briefly stick. In spite of all
the drive-by viewers and daily tourist
boodles. There's an even loftier peg
deep in this newer bashful
digs by the lake. Something
which gibes & jibs at Mr. Gross,
wanting only to build, re-build

& then subtract his British bricks.
Windy city's always looking for a
fresher tarmac, wishing to build
in open, less upholstered ways.

More peculiar to the talents of
her undo prairies. Not of parliaments.
Keeping no honored, lasting courts;
or that which will suffer centuries once
consecrated by a throne.

iii.

TRAVEL, go venture beyond, a pair of
Lloyd Wright homes. An Adler
or Sullivan frame, or maybe a few
terra cotta water tower deposit zones.
This is the way we princely

honor over here, a towne which
first curtsied the sky, then over
and over again kept praising
the royal district above, to rise
and rise up in lightening rods.

Not scepters. Always to make
demolishing, treasonous switches,
then to start all over again.
Only these, and few samples still
bare witness. A lost Chicago—and proud.

iv.
THIS seems to work against all
European logic; all safe home-towne
neighborhood facts. Against every
lasting legacy. Tempting the welcome,
and, then the exit of all visual empires.

v.
BUT still, we dare not choose to
Supplant, nor to breed any more of this,
our lovely Alta Vista Terrace.
Curious guests and local droppers
must arrive, savor and drive by daily,

stopping to sign our royal, lasting charter.
Helping us relish and ransom a former home
away from home, our open victory absent
from the sky. We won it from our adopted cousins
over there. On the London side of the tracks.

THE ALLERTON

tip top tap
The old club hotel
still watches all things afar on
the Mag Mile
below.

tip top tap
She's left her swanky
cocktails to ghosts,
with Donny Mc Neil sitting in the
breakfast club
above.

tip top tap
In the air her many
spirits carve stone details,
Murgatroyd & Ogden still jotting down
behind the walls along
her wired stage
beyond.

tip top tap
Is only part . . . tapped now.

Her cornerstone from '24
still calls her to heaven, but
without her *petit dejeuner*, nor her daily
devotional petition. And she
makes no daily calls to Fran in
the clouds so close to her
above.

No more prayers will
avail any of them higher up, or
we here below, as Sirius
passes over all by
and by:

So the air waves will boast no top,
So the drinks will cover no tap,
So the breakfast leaves no tip.
And now we keep all our broadcasts . . . *ad libitum*.

LAKEVIEW CATHLEEN

I.
Only on chosen days
　　　Will the mid-summer
Wind Rocket around the

　　　Tabled side walks. Arriving
Quickly, it trims the neighborhood
　　　With a stiff yardstick,
Which forces tight parking,

And then something special takes
　　　Place, smack at the
Corner, boldly in broad face
　　　Of the coffee, Caribou!

At that very moment all
　　　Befalls a silent *Al fresco,*
As Cathy arrives and takes
　　　Her throne. As she, from her
Little iron bench, prepares

To watch very long
　　　Chins and grim faces,
From a nearby
　　　Wrigley death at home.

As the flocks and flocks
　　　Of cheerless Cubby blues,
Leave their wake, Cathy sits
　　　And sits crossed legged.
She simply sizzles and waits.

She knows how baseball
      Curses promptly; and forces
Its divine will by Chicago design.
      So with her vast sun glasses

And steamy hot legs, Cathy
      Gently flicks her cigarette,
Sips her cup, with lady-like
      Perch, then continues to
unwind. She knows how fans
      Will soon pass by, some bogus-unaware.
      She knows how they're nosy,
And how they pine to snap a manly
      Glance. And stare. How they nudge

Their girl friend's and giggle. But Cathy
      Just sits and sits there, dressed
To the nines and sizzles.

II.

Cathy's black bench
      Rests not far from colorful
Blossoms, and common ferns,
      And brighter beds of roses.
Around the bend she sees
      How gay squirrels hoard for

Pristine condos. How older men
      Keep drooling. How they struggle to talk
Younger, while buzzing like bees.
      She watches how the heart of

Broadway is ever so fattened
      With shirtless curbside boys.
And so she sits there sexy to
      The nines, just being and sizzling,

And watching, full poise.
      Cathy knows hotter rivalry
Will never fail, they'll always, ever
      Soften hearts. Whimsical with

Shirtless torsos, the better treats of
      Garden shows, they have perennial
Pollen cycles. More redolent flowers than she.
      But, her Manhattan savvy knows all

Of this. That the season of passion and
      Plants will always
Come and go—like baseball.
      Or summer days which come and
Quit like clockwork—how only *magic* is on her side.

III.

But who can say when Cathy will ever
      Show up again? The numbered
Days of Ward 44's sunlight can never
      Promise her pending thrill. You see

Cathy's really a singular, savvy kind
      Of neighborhood guy. And she's been

Duped by the diehards of this Midwestern town.
      In their windy city twill, some
Love to label her a drag, a freak, even a queer
      Gangster. But Cathy's really a

New York Bob with a mind, and a motive. A cheerful
      Prankster. He's self confident, he's
Really a joyful set of clothes, never far from
      Imagination—and Cathy's elder, wiser

Brother, Though he too wears her hot legs
       Often to be hidden. He knows he's
No prince, no hunk, no idol. He senses
       How 'sis' is quite lovelier when
Donning her bracelets, fishnets and glossy boots.

He knows Cathy's spicy, how she sizzles sitting on her
       Black iron bench. So he's always present too,
Defending his mother's blood, his hotter North side wench.
       You see Lakeview Cathy's no lady wannabe, no

'Sicko', and she's certainly no faux. She's kind, sultry and bright,
       She's only her brother's hoax of a Midwestern delight.

Cathy's always stage inclusive, she's a fun to be seen.
       A hidden treasure and always something singular, in between.

CHICAGO'S OWN CENTURY

Just give us a bit more of your clock,
A few more, longer seconds for lawful growth,
And this century's ours for the taking. Bounteous.
        Big bad hearted, with a touch of the old
        Imperial Capone.

Our great prairies shred apart no edges, hold no limits for
Themselves. Not bottled, skirted sweat like east coast islets. Our perspiration
Cannot be contained; our burned down city keeps combusting from the lake.
        Reinventing is always on demand
        As given.

Structural chronicle is for timed wrenches. The past is an exchange for us.
It will always be tomorrow. Departing history must always be confronted.
Our water tables have no lasting seeds in onion fields and glacier sideboards,
        So when we develop windy city produce it grows old
        And spoils.

We keep cutting our losses from the past by giving birth to newer sky
Scrapers, bluer collars, mixed neighborhoods and La Salle Street rising from the lake.
We're not anything once colonial or pyrotechnic, or really a braggart of sorts.
        Just a casual matter of marked genes of who we will
        Always become.

CPSIA information can be obtained at www.ICGtesting.com
Printed in the USA
242863LV00003B/130/P